I0439856

ViewCaps Presents:

Immigration

The Pros and Cons of the Issue

BOOKCAPS

BookCaps™ Study Guides

www.bookcaps.com

Cover Image © kozini - Fotolia.com

Table of Contents

About ViewCaps

ViewCaps is an imprint of BookCaps™ Study Guides. Each book in this series presents a current event or topic in a non-biased way and let's you decide what you believe about the issue. You can find more books in the series by visiting our website: **www.bookcaps.com**.

Introduction: Why Immigration Matters

The United States is a melting pot. A large number of immigrants live in the United States and come here from all over the planet, through both legal and illegal methods. Often, groups that encourage immigration cite the fact that the United States is a diverse, wonderful mixture of people who contribute to the flavor of the American culture. In America, immigration is the primary cause for population increases. The number of immigrants is exploding. Every year, over 2.5 million immigrants enter the United States. A million immigrants enter legally while 1.5 million enter illegally. More than a quarter of all minors (people under the age of 18) are immigrants. The most immigrants come to the United States from Mexico, China, the Philippines, India, Cuba, and Colombia[i]. In 2006, more people immigrated to the United States than to the rest of the world put together. America is seen as a highly desirable place to live in. There are high chances of employment and social mobility, and good opportunities for higher education and superior medical care. Above all, it is a good place to escape to when avoiding political oppression. When choosing where to live, immigrants are more likely to live among people of a similar cultural background. There are several reasons for this phenomenon. Immigrants are often poorer than native-born citizens and settle in poorer neighborhoods where communication and transportation costs are lower (due to the availability of public transportation). Another reason is the fact that having linguistic similarities makes it easier for community members to share information.

Because there are so many people who enter the United States every year, American culture is continually changing and warping. The social, political, and economic implications of immigration vary substantially from community to community. For that reason, some groups encourage immigration while others discourage it. Those who feel the negative consequences of immigration tend to advocate for harsher regulations against it while those who benefit from it tend to advocate leniency towards immigrants. After the September 11 attacks, public opinion about immigration changed from more positive to more negative. Before the attacks, over 60% of Americans believed that immigration was good for the country. After the attacks, only 50% believed the same. Furthermore, 55% of Americans favored lowering the cap on legal immigration. Immigrants have experienced a change in attitude by Americans towards them after the attacks. Twenty-four percent of immigrants reported that they felt discriminated against[ii]. Americans feel more favorably towards immigrated residents who have lived in the country for a long time and have established strong communities, like the Italians, Jews, and Poles. They tend to feel less favorably towards those who are more recent immigrants, like

Mexican immigrants because they feel that the older generations of immigrants have contributed more positively to American culture and assimilated better.[iii]

Although some groups see legal immigration in a favorable light, most see illegal immigration as something that needs to be reformed and regulated. Legal immigrants are seen as hard-working people who follow the rules to get to the American Dream while illegal immigrants are seen as drains on the American society. Most immigrants view the United States as a place where anyone can achieve their dreams with hard work and dedication; such is the American Dream. The American Dream helps describe why immigration has grown so dramatically in the past few decades. As the nation's GDP increases, and as Americans get wealthier on average over time, more immigrants see the United States as a good place to live and prosper.[iv]

Part I: Immigration - For

Chapter 1: Groups that Favor Immigration

Several groups favor immigration for a plethora of often conflicting reasons. A lot of ethnic groups favor immigration because they seek to support members of their own ethnicity when they immigrate to the United States. Often, immigrants arrive to the United States poorer than the average American resident. They are in need of moral support, housing, English education, and culture education. Although some ethnic groups are willing to provide this kind of support, most other pro-immigration support immigration for purely economic or political reasons.

Republicans for Immigration Reform (RIR)

This organization is an "independent-expenditure only committee." In other words, this Republican group does not make any contributions to a candidate's campaign unless they follow the same ideologies that the donors do. Besides providing funds to specific electoral campaigns, RIR funds research and sponsors legislation that are in line with their goals. Their goals are purely economical and political in nature; RIR argues that immigration, both legal and illegal, benefits the American economy and that being in favor of immigration can help improve their party's opportunities among Hispanic voters, who tend to favor Democratic candidates. RIR warn that not appealing to immigrants would render their party permanently weak and in the minority. They also promise fellow Republicans, who tend to advocate for stronger immigrations laws, that RIR will always push for first securing the border, then inviting more immigrants into the United States. They seek to "repair the damage left by years of anti-illegal-immigrant rhetoric that has dominated GOP primaries and alienated crucial Hispanic voters."[v]

RIR is primarily composed of entrepreneurs and businessmen. They put pressure on the federal government to allow more highly skilled immigrants into the United States, as their skills are often needed for growing businesses. Additionally, RIR argues, immigration laws stop entrepreneurs from coming into the United States. They argue that the immigration of additional entrepreneurs will be tremendously beneficial to the United States' economy because such businessmen are highly educated and innovative, and their business schemes create jobs for American citizens and permanent residents. They also seek to reform immigration so that immigrants can stay in the United States for a longer period of time and continue to grow their businesses.[vi]

One of the bills that RIR has been advocating is the Startup Act 2.0. This piece of legislation seeks to create two new types of permanent residence visas to invite intelligent, job-creating workers to the United States: one for foreign students who seek masters and doctorate degrees in science- and math-related fields, and the other for immigrants who start successful businesses in the United States, but only if they hire American workers and raise at least $100,000 in capital prior to immigration. This act would also modify the tax code to encourage investors to invest in newer businesses. RIR argues that the government only gives out 65,000 visas to high-skilled immigrants, yet employers (in 2012) submitted almost 375,000 applications, even though the submitting process takes a lot of effort and time on the companies' part. [vii]

Another thing that RIR advocates for is bringing low-skilled immigrants in from Mexico as guest workers during harvest season to pick food crops. This measure used to exist from 1942 to 1964, during World War II, when the United States experienced a shortage of low-skilled labor. RIR argues that this measure would help curb illegal immigration. Furthermore, immigration from Mexico can be more easily regulated and would, as a result, be much safer for the immigrants themselves. And instead of sitting around and waiting for the harvest season to start, immigrants can be sent back to Mexico. This can help reduce some of the stress law enforcers feel as resentment and restlessness increase among unemployed illegal immigrants during the off-season time. [viii]

No More Deaths

This organization is purely humanitarian. It started when a few religious groups got together and decided to take action against the higher number of casualties taking place near the Mexican border. Illegal immigrants are often ignorant of the hardships that travelers face when journeying into the United States. No More Deaths says that thousands of men, women, and children die when trying to cross the harsh Sonoran Desert. In 1990, only nine illegal immigrants died while walking into the United States. In 2005, the number of dead shot up to more 500. No More Deaths says that there may actually be more deaths because counts do not include the bodies of those who are never found. Eighty percent of the dead were immigrants who were under forty years old. Each year, more and more immigrants under the age of eighteen die while crossing the border.[ix]

Religious leaders from the Catholic, Jewish, and Presbyterian communities came together to help stop these deaths. Hundreds of volunteers got together in the summer to offer food, water, and medical aid to those who had recently crossed the border. In the summer, the death toll is especially high because of the intense heat of the Sonoran desert. Volunteers working with No More Deaths drive through the desert to look for hurt immigrants. They also patrol the desert on foot around the clock and set up permanent camps to offer food and medical aid to anyone who needs it. The reason that No More Deaths focuses on the desert is because they know that illegal immigrants often avoid urban areas for fear of getting caught and jailed. Besides directly engaging in concrete humanitarian efforts, No More Deaths also seeks to advocate for immigration reform. Specifically, they argue that militarizing the border and making it so strong against immigrants leads to more deaths than is necessary. They say that border patrol units scare immigrants to cross at places where crossing takes much longer and is much more dangerous. This group saves about 160 people per year.[x]

National Council of La Raza

There are plenty of Hispanic American groups that are dedicated to eliminating the wealth and education gaps between Hispanic immigrants and the remaining population of the United States. National Council of La Raza, in particular, is concerned with the fact that Mexican Americans face many obstacles as a result of their relative poverty. This organization is "the largest Hispanic civil rights and advocacy organization in the United States."[xi] It seeks to help Hispanic Americans, especially recent immigrants. It conducts research, analyzes policies, and then advocates their stance to government officials after meeting with Hispanic community leaders. NCLR researches all kinds of policies, ranging from investments, immigration, civil rights, and the health, economic, and education status of Hispanic Americans. Their research pertains to the health of the Latino community; if legislation is favorable to their community, they urge community members to vote for it. If policies are not favorable to their community, they lobby lawmakers and inform them about Latino sentiment. It seeks to provide opportunities to individuals who need support after coming to the United States. NCLR helps legal immigrants get settled. It helps them find lawyers, make decisions when voting and buying homes, find job opportunities, housing, and healthcare services. It also helps them find classes to educate themselves about American systems and the English language. NCLR is especially concerned with working with youth, as they believe in justice for juveniles and youth leadership. They organize several literacy programs that encourage the youth to apply to colleges and parents to stay involved in their children's future. Through all these programs, NCLR makes adjusting to a new life in a new country easier.

NCLR is often accused of supporting illegal immigration because it does not discriminate when assisting members of the Hispanic community, even in matters like purchasing a home. It provides social services to illegal immigrants who have "anchor babies." This matter will be discussed in greater detail in the section titled "Children." NCLR, however, denies supporting illegal immigration and states that it respects the United States' sovereignty above all. They also cite their consistent advocacy for more effective border control to show that they only seek to help legal immigrants.[xii]

Chapter 2: Arguments For

Positive Economic Effects of Immigration

It's difficult to study the economic effects of immigration, especially illegal immigration. This is because such effects are complex. Often, one effect sets off a chain of other, seemingly unrelated effects that are difficult to predict. For example, an argument that is commonly made is that illegal immigration depresses the wage for low-skilled workers in the United States. Pro-immigration groups counter with the fact that the overall cost of goods is also depressed by illegal immigration, making the economic pros and cons of illegal immigration roughly equivalent. It is difficult to calculate the exact depression in costs of goods[xiii]. For that reason, it is impossible to say whether immigration is purely good or purely bad for the United States economy. Other groups argue that illegal immigrants have a small, net positive, negligible effect on the American economy. These groups argue that the net effect of other trends are much, much larger and have a much greater impact on the economy than an influx of illegal immigrants, like the price of oil and the climate in agricultural areas. It is, however, easier to ascertain other effects that immigrants have on the economy, like total wage depression, cost of services, and total taxes paid. Using these facts, we can see whether immigrants are "good" or "bad" for the economy. We must make judgments about which of these indicators of economic health we will choose to look at. An overwhelming majority of economists believe that immigration (legal and illegal) is beneficial to the economy.[xiv]

Often, anti-immigration groups claim that a big influx of legal (and illegal), low-income immigrants causes wage depression of all low-wage workers nationwide. In response to such arguments, the National Research Council reports that all the arguments made by anti-immigration groups are made suggestively, with no concrete data to back up claims while hard, collected data shows that low-wage workers are not hit by depressed wages because immigration does not depress wages. The argument that blacks suffer particularly due to job competition from low-skilled immigrants is also addressed in their report. The National Research Council maintains that blacks do not feel particularly hard-hit by immigrant influxes because their communities are located far away from immigrant communities. The report further argues that black communities' wages depend on entirely different factors.[xv] Even cities located just above the border do not feel wage depression due to illegal immigration. Groups in favor of immigration argue that the effect of illegal immigration on wages is exaggerated.[xvi]

Several anti-immigration groups (discussed later on in this guide) claim that immigration, both legal and legal, take away jobs from native-born American citizens. This claim is not based on data. Increased immigration levels have not hindered Americans' abilities to find jobs.[xvii] In fact, if we look at the numbers, immigrants make up 15% of the labor force in the United States. Twenty-one million immigrants hold jobs in America. The number of unemployed workers, on the other hand, is only 7 million.[xviii] Therefore, it is illogical to assume that all jobs previously held by unemployed American workers are now held by immigrant workers.

Furthermore, immigration creates jobs, both directly and indirectly. Before coming into the United States, individuals and families have to apply to the United States Citizenship and Immigration Services (USCIS). The USCIS is 99% funded by immigration application fees.[xix] In other words, individuals from around the world create almost all of the 18,000 jobs that the federal employees at the USCIS hold.[xx] According to research conducted by Dr. Raul Hinojosa-Ojeda, approximately 8 million American jobs held by American citizens are created by economic activity produced by illegal immigrants alone.[xxi] The economic effects of the spending habits of *legal* immigrants are no doubt, more positive because legal immigrants make more money on average than their illegal counterparts. Legal immigrants are seen as a source of economic prosperity. On average, entrepreneurial activity is almost 40% higher in legal immigrants than for

American-born citizens.[xxii] There are over 1.6 million Hispanic immigrant- owned businesses.[xxiii] Immigrants are also heavily involved with the founding and maintaining of several large American corporations, including Google, Yahoo, and eBay.

Immigrants are also often more educated than native-born Americans. In fact while the immigrant population makes up only 12.5% of the total United States population[xxiv], more than forty percent of PhD holders in the United States are immigrants.[xxv] Immigrants, on average, boost demand for goods, increase economic productivity, depress the price of necessities, and are highly innovative and motivated individuals.[xxvi]

Although anti-immigrant sentiment is high in cities where there are a large number of unemployed people,[xxvii] illegal immigrant labor is used heavily in the agricultural industry. Businesses who actually hire illegal immigrants (such as farm owners and other sectors of the agricultural industry) argue that Americans don't want to do the jobs that illegal immigrants do.[xxviii] Most Americans agree. In a New York Times poll, over 53% of American citizens said that "illegal immigrants mostly take the jobs Americans don't want."[xxix] According to Ernesto Zedillo, the former Mexican President and the Director of the Yale Center for the Study of Globalization, the American economy needs illegal immigrants. He backs his argument with the fact that illegal immigration follows a seasonal pattern. Illegal immigration is often high just before harvest seasons because fruit-picking jobs are easily available.[xxx] Historically, illegal immigration has always been higher than legal immigration. Yet after the recession of 2008, these trends reversed and the number of illegal immigrants working in this country dropped dramatically.[xxxi] This fact supports Zedillo's claim: Illegal immigration is fueled by demand for cheap labor.

If laws were to get stricter with regards to illegal immigration (for instance, if all employers had to verify and report the legal statuses of their workers), and all illegal immigrants were to be removed from the United States' workforce, several industries would collapse because they would face a severe shortage of workers. To mitigate their collapse, economists theorize that Americans would have to take up the "undesirable" jobs normally done by illegal workers and do work that is far below their skill and education level. To attract workers to these "undesirable" jobs, employers would have to hike their wages. Economists argue that this would be disastrous for the American economy because the prices of goods would rise, rendering the escalated wages meaningless on a material scale. This would cause rampant inflation and would kill the competitiveness of American industries on a global scale.[xxxii]

Besides the fact that there is so much demand for cheap labor in the United States (see section HB87 for a detailed description of economic effects of and demand for illegal immigrant labor in the state of

Georgia), all of the advantages that are associate with using cheap labor are the employers', who are almost always American citizens. Employers do not have to pay as much in wages to illegal immigrants because they do not demand as much as legal workers. They also do not have to pay the costs that are associated with hiring legal workers, like welfare contributions and other non-wage costs.[xxxiii] Therefore, the argument can be made that illegal immigration is directly beneficial to American citizens working in the agricultural industry. The money that is made in profits by employers is pushed into the American economy by way of spending. The money that illegal immigrants make also gets pushed into the American economy. Almost all the money that illegal immigrants make is spent immediately.

Illegal Immigration Cost to Services Analysis

One of the biggest arguments that anti-immigration groups make with respect to illegal immigrants is the claim that illegal immigrants are drains on the American system of services. Such groups claim that illegal immigrants take out more in services than they give back because they do not pay income taxes. However, this premise is based on a false statement. Illegal immigrants do pay taxes. In fact, illegal immigrants contribute more in taxes than they take out in services, including health care, social security, education, and other social welfare services.[xxxiv] Over

6 million illegal immigrants pay income taxes every year because they work under a randomized, bogus social security number that gets written into the social security system. Anywhere from between 50% to 75% of all illegal immigrants work with bogus social security numbers. (When looking at this statistic, it's important to note that a large number of illegal immigrants are children who do not hold jobs. This number, "50 to 75%" does not represent the percentage of working illegal immigrants.) In Texas, in 2006, illegal immigrants paid almost $18 billion in taxes while only taking away only $1.2 billion in state services.[xxxv]

Critics of anti-immigration groups claim that even if illegal immigrants did take in more in services than they pay in income tax, they fit in with citizens of similar economic standing. In fact, 60% of Americans take in more in services than they pay in taxes simply because the wealthiest Americans pay the most in income tax; thirty-seven percent of federal income taxes come from the wealthiest 1% of Americans.[xxxvi] The average immigrant (both legal and illegal), however, pays $80,000 more in taxes than they receive in services.[xxxvii] This is because both legal and illegal immigration is set up such that net taxation is maximized.

To understand the argument that illegal immigrants put in more into tax systems than they take out, it's important to look at the Social Security system. In order to understand how this concept makes sense, it is important to understand how the social security system works. Every month, Americans pay a percentage of their monthly income and receive all the benefits back when they turn sixty-five years old. This works as a sort of mandatory retirement plan that the government handles. The government keeps the money and often invests in governmental activities. This allows the savings to circulate within the economy, which is beneficial because it increases economic activity and creates jobs. Pro-immigration groups often cite the fact that the social security system (which almost all senior American citizens depend on for their sustenance) is held up by illegal immigration. In other words, if illegal immigrants did not make the $7 billion in social security payments every year, the entire social security system would certainly collapse. This happens because illegal immigrants pay taxes when they use false social security numbers. They do not, however, receive the benefits associated with these payments when they turn sixty-five years old because they are illegal aliens. The contributions that they make add up to about 10% of surplus funds in the social security system every year. This difference is significant because it represents the difference between how much money is given away to senior legal Americans and the amount of money that is received in payments. In other words, if illegal immigrants were not paying this money, senior citizens would not get any benefits. Groups in favor of immigration argue that inviting more illegal immigrants by relaxing control on the border would boost the declining health of the social security system. Because the number of illegal immigrants has been slowly increasing since the 1990s (there were over 9 million W-2's filed with bogus social security numbers in 2002), the amount of money the Social Security system gets every year is also increasing. The money that illegal immigrants put in not only generates approximately $7 billion in Social Security revenue, but also $1.5 billion in Medicare revenue that is used to provide elderly Americans with health insurance. To better understand how illegal immigrants were contributing to Social Security finances, Social Security actuaries created a simulation which increased net illegal immigration from 900,000 per year (the assumed influx of illegal immigrants to the United States who contributed in taxes) to 1.3 million a year. They found that their system would save half a trillion dollars over the system's 75-year funding gap. The problem with Social Security today is that more and more money is given away every year than collected (because Americans have been living longer, and the baby-boom generation is reaching retirement age). Allowing in 400,000 more illegal immigrants into the United States would close the gap between spending and earning, according to Social Security estimates.[xxxviii]

Anti-immigration groups often argue that illegal immigrants take away precious medical attention from doctors who would otherwise be servicing legal immigrants and American citizens. The argument is often made that illegal immigrants slow down emergency rooms and are taking away Medicaid from people who are here legally. This argument is not based on concrete facts. Neither legal nor illegal immigrants are eligible for Medicaid. Legal immigrants may become eligible only after staying in the country for more than five years and filing a claim for it. It is true, however, that illegal immigrants who get hit by an emergency can receive some basic Medicaid coverage, but only if they are children, pregnant women, elderly, or disabled. But to say that they "drain" the health system is simply not true, because the cost of emergency care represents only 1% of Medicaid costs. The other 99% goes to providing health care and medication for American citizens.[xxxix] Furthermore, immigrants are often much healthier than native-born Americans. This is because they are younger, stronger, and mentally healthier because they cope better with stress. Unhealthier people are less likely to migrate.[xl]

It is important to remember that the data given with respect to Social Security and Medicaid might not be perfect indicators of how much illegal immigrants contribute and take away in services. For one thing, costs of educating the children of illegal immigrants were not factored into the calculations. Illegal immigration poses additional costs on the American tax system. For example, criminal activity (crossing the border illegally and other crimes) represents a cost to law enforcement agencies. However, even if immigration caused a net loss in the American tax system, it still provides a net gain to the American economy because with high rates of illegal immigration, pay for high-skilled workers in the United States increases, the price of goods and services produced by immigration decreases, and the economic system gets more efficient in terms of wages and owning capital. Simply put, economic activity initiated by illegal immigrants creates so many American jobs that the net benefits far outweigh the net costs.[xli]

Criminal Activity in the Immigrant Population

One of the most common misconceptions perpetuated by anti-immigration groups is that crime rates are higher among immigrant populations than native-borns. This propaganda is simply untrue. The percentage of immigrants in jail is much, much lower than the percentage of immigrants in the community. For example, within United States, California has the largest immigrant population. Approximately 35% of Californians are immigrants, but immigrants represent only 17% of the prison population. Furthermore, native-born adult men are imprisoned at a rate that is 2.5 times greater than the rate of imprisonment of immigrants.

There are various reasons why immigrants are underrepresented in American prison populations. Firstly, immigrants have a strong incentive to behave according to the law for fear of deportation. Secondly, legal immigrants also investigated for criminal activity before they are allowed to enter the United States. Third, from 1998 to 2008, over 800,000 immigrants (both legal and illegal) were deported.

Therefore, the number of immigrant criminals still left in prisons is smaller than the number that would be if deportation was not used as a punishment. The fourth reason is a consequence of the third one; immigrants who are deported cannot come back to the United States. Therefore, networks of criminal activity are broken, and fewer members of that community get incarcerated. Lastly, immigrants have lived in the United States for a shorter period of time, which gives them less time to commit crimes.[xlii]

In certain immigrant communities, crime rates are higher than those of the native-born population. To learn why this happens, see the section in the next chapter titled "Crime in the Illegal Immigrant Community."

Refugees - Giving shelter to those who need it

One of the biggest benefits of immigration is the fact that United States allows refugees to enter and live here peacefully. Refugees, as dictated by International Law, can gain legal status by seeking and receiving asylum in United States. Individuals can be given refugee status either by entering the United States and requesting asylum upon arrival, or applying for refugee status while still abroad. Refugees are different from "regular" immigrants who seek to enter the United States for economic or family-related reasons because refugees have a higher chance of getting accepted into the United States. It is still not easy to enter the United States as a refugee; the application is still vigorous. In 2008, the United States granted asylum to a record-breaking 80,000 people. Since 1975, the United States admitted more than 1.3 million Asians immigrants as refugees. The refugee population makes up less than 10% of all immigrants admitted to the United States yearly. Although refugees are accepted from all over the world, significant refugee populations come from Somalia, Liberia, Sudan, Bhutan, Iraq, and Ethiopia.[xliii]

One of the strongest pro-immigration arguments commonly made by ethnicity-based organizations and humanitarian groups is the fact that allowing refugees to claim asylum is a humane practice. Without asylum, many people who could otherwise live normal lives may end up getting hurt in a hostile community. The United States boasts that it admits the largest number of refugees annually. While approximately 80,000 people are granted asylum by the United States, Canada gives only 25,000 similar status, the United Kingdom only 30,000, and Japan a measly 41 people per year.[xliv] To gain asylum, refugees must prove the following:[xlv]

    1.   They fear persecution.

    2.   They are getting persecuted because of race, religion, nationality, political opinion, or social group.

3.   The government of the country they live in or the state to which they belong cannot control the persecution, or is involved in the persecution.

Illegal Immigrant Children

An argument that groups in favor of immigration, social service groups, and humanitarian groups often make is one that revolves around the children of illegal immigrants. Such groups claim that illegal immigrants' children have no choice and are brought into the country when they are far too young to truly understand the consequences, especially that they are breaking the law. Therefore, these groups argue that law enforcement officials should be more lenient with illegal immigrant family members, especially immigrant children. Children that are born in the United States to illegal immigrants are stuck in even more of a predicament. Their parents should be, by law, deported, but they are American citizens, so they cannot be. Federal courts and the Immigration and Naturalization Service refuse to delay the deportation of illegal immigrants simply because they have American citizen children in the country. Sometimes, the results can be heartbreaking, especially if the children are young.[xlvi] Over three million American citizens have at least one illegal immigrant parent. Over 13,000 American children had their parents deported from 2005 to 2007.[xlvii]

There have been several cases of American citizens that were so young, the deportation of their mothers caused much trauma and distress. La Raza denounced the separation of a nursing mother from her baby in 2007. An illegal immigrant named Saida Umanzor was taken to jail while she waited to be deported. While there, her breasts clogged up painfully with milk that she was not giving her nine month old daughter, Brittney Bejarano. She and her daughter suffered tremendously because the separation; her daughter was not consuming much else besides her mother's milk at the time. The separation was painful for them both. After more than three days in jail, and after much petitioning, La Raza was able to get Umanzor a breast pump to help her relieve herself. Meanwhile, her baby was placed under the care of social workers. (For a detailed discussion of La Raza, please visit the section about groups in favor of immigration.) The case of Umanzor is not uncommon. Over 8% of children born in the United States are born to illegal immigrants. Separation of nursing mothers from their young, often newborn children is something that immigration authorities are faced with in the United States. To deal with such complex situations, immigration authorities struggle to work as quickly, justly, and humanely as possible. Such cases became more relevant during and after the Bush administration. The Bush administration pushed the strictest enforcement of immigration laws. Under the Bush administration, the deportation of illegal immigrants escalated dramatically. This trend continued into the Obama administration. Anti-illegal immigration groups often argue that parents put their children in such painful situations by breaking the law. They cite the fact that even American citizens are faced with separation from their young if they break the law. However, as Umanroz's case was publicized by the media, more women's health groups and humanitarian organizations began denouncing separation of newborn children from their nursing mothers. In 2007, the Immigration and Customs Enforcement Agency released more lenient guidelines about nursing mothers. It allowed them to remain out of jail unless they are a threat to national security.[xlviii]

According to research done by La Raza, two-thirds of children born to illegal immigrants were born in the United States. They are motivated to give birth in the United States because they want their children to become American citizens. (For a more detailed discussion of "anchor babies," please see the section titled "Illegal Immigrant Children" in the next chapter of this guide.) Anti-immigration groups argue that the practice of giving citizenship to all children born in the United States, regardless of their parents' legal status, has been encouraging illegal immigration. Such groups say that illegal immigrants rationalize that they will not be as hard hit by the law as those who do not have children, simply because their children are American citizens. However, humanitarian organizations argue that deportation and separation of mothers who have otherwise not broken the law is cruel. The deportation of parents is a real and common phenomena. In 2007, in just one month, immigration officials raided three factories for illegal immigrants and arrested 912 adults to be deported. They had 506 children between them, 340 under the age of ten. The majority of these children were American citizens who were taken up by social services while their parents were shipped out of the country. To escape deportation, families often hide in their basements for days at a time.[xlix]

Deportation of their parents causes tremendous damage to children. Not only do they face emotional distress, they also face severe economic hardship. Often, such children live with their relatives who are afraid to ask the government for some assistance to raise them, despite the fact that they are citizens, simply because other relatives may be illegal immigrants in fear of deportation. Because these children are American citizens, much debate has centered on them. While anti-immigration groups argue that it is much too easy for people to become citizens, groups in favor of immigration, like La Raza, argue that laws actually need to become more lenient. There are several solutions to the problem that partially illegal immigrant families pose to the United States. Some suggest to do away with granting children citizenship at all. Then when time comes, the entire family can be united in their deportation. This solution has been deemed unconstitutional on several counts because it violates the Bill of Rights, which grants all individuals born on American soil the gift of citizenship. Other groups advocate giving parents of US citizens citizenship so that the whole family can live in the United States together. Anti-immigration groups argue that giving green cards or citizenship away so easily would be unfair to those who work hard to get to the United States legally. They also claim that this would encourage more people to break the law.[l] However, economists say that it might be beneficial to grant citizenship, or at least legal status, to undocumented immigrants with children. They argue that legalization would improve children's chances of success and becoming educated, productive taxpayers.[li]

Although the Obama administration has been regulating immigration and deportation laws strictly, Obama has granted certain provisions to illegal immigrants. Under his administration, illegal immigrant parents are allowed to "work, travel, and send their kids to school without fear of deportation while they wait to apply for green cards. No federal benefits, no vote, but no sword of Damocles either."[lii] On 4 March 2013, he also passed a memorandum that allows illegal immigrants to stay in the United States if they can prove that separation from their American citizen children, spouses, or parents would put them through extensive hardships. They can also apply for visas without leaving the United States, but only if they have lived in the United States for at least ten years, and have good moral character. Groups in favor of immigration and humanitarian groups have showed strong support for these laws because it can help parents avoid the situation that Saida Umanzor went through.[liii]

Chapter 3: Important Legal Cases and Legislation

Deferred Action for Childhood Arrivals (DACA)

Several measures have been brought up to make it easier for immigrants who come to the United States illegally at a young age with their parents. Groups in favor of immigration claim that these children are faultless because they are not aware that they are breaking the law. They have no choice but to accompany their parents. Such groups suggest that the path to citizenship be made easier for such children.

Obama passed this memorandum on 15 June 2012. A memorandum is passed by executive action. In other words, the Senate and the House of Representatives have no say in its passage. Through this memorandum, Obama instructed Customs and Border Protection, Citizenship and Immigration Services, and Immigration and Customs Enforcement not to deport illegal immigrant children who were not hurting the American society. The DACA allows children to live in the United States for two years without facing any kind of prosecution. It also allows them to submit applications to temporarily work under United States employers. Obama passed this memorandum after the DREAM Act (the Development, Relief, and Education for Alien Minors Act) failed. The DREAM Act initially aimed to make it easier for illegal immigrant children to assimilate into American society. Children who arrived in the United States before age 16, lived within United States borders for five consecutive years, graduated from an American high school, and taken at least two years of higher education or served in the military for at least two years would be eligible to apply for a green card. Unfortunately for illegal immigrant college students, this act failed. Critics of this law argued vehemently against it, saying that it would attract more illegal immigrants to bring their children to the United States. They also criticized that it was unfair to students who had to pay the full cost of tuition because the DREAM Act allowed illegal immigrant children to receive federal aid. They further argued that the DREAM Act would protect gang members from deportation, as all they would have to do to avoid deportation is show officials some documents which proved their attendance in a community college.[liv]

Under DACA, the USCIS established rules about who could enjoy the benefits that this memorandum offered, and who would get deported. Children could only stay in the United States for two years if they qualified. They could, however, renew their reprieve from deportation by undergoing the vigorous application process again. DACA does not give green cards or citizenship to children. They are only allowed to work under U.S. employers if they can show that they would face economic hardship by remaining unemployed. Although this law is strict, it still allows children relief from deportation. Furthermore, it does not apply to children who come to the United States after 2012, disproving opponents of this memorandum who claim it would encourage more illegal immigration. Although Democrats and groups in favor of immigration support this memorandum, Republicans remain divided. States too, have not formed a consensus when applying this law into their own state law.[lv] In California, for example, an "illegal-immigrant friendly" state, individuals who receive a DACA grant are allowed to get a driver's license as long as they pay income taxes. Arizona, on the other hand, a state that enforces anti-immigration laws strictly, refused to grant any state benefits to DACA beneficiaries. Maryland, on the other hand, went above and beyond to welcoming illegal immigrant children. Any child who went to a Maryland high school and whose parents paid taxes regularly are eligible for in-state tuition when attending college. Maryland officials also refuse to ask anyone about their legal status.[lvi]

HB 87

One of the harshest immigration laws that was passed in the United States was The Arizona Senate Bill 1070. (For more information about this law, see the section in the next chapter labeled "Arizona Senate Bill 1070.") This bill enforces federal immigration laws strictly, deporting any and all immigrants caught without proper documentation. The passage of this law encouraged several other states to pass similar laws. Georgia, for example, passed the HB 87 in 2011. This law also initiated the stricter enforcement of federal anti-immigration laws. It became criminal for immigrants to work with false documents (including bogus social security numbers). It also became illegal for people to transport illegal immigrants within the state boundaries of Georgia, give illegal immigrants shelter, or encourage more illegal immigration to Georgia. This law is heavily criticized by humanitarian groups because it makes no allowances for transport of illegal immigrants even if it is for emergency situations, or if the transporter (such as a bus driver) simply was not aware of the passenger's legal status. This law also makes no allowances for universities, hospitals, and churches which shelter illegal immigrants, even unknowingly. Like the Arizona State Law, this law requires law enforcement officials to ask people about their legal status. It also requires all employers who work with ten or more workers to use a software called "E-Verify" to check the legal status of all their employees.[lvii]

Several civil rights groups have protested vehemently to HB 87. Like the Arizona State Bill, they say it encourages racial profiling. Racial profiling is unconstitutional because it does not guarantee everyone the same due process during criminal prosecution. La Raza, in particular, published guidelines about what to do when a police pulls you over to ask for legal status. Police often ask people who they pull over questions, like "Where are you from?" Based on their responses, they demand verification of legal status. Groups claim that this practice is illegal and racist. La Raza encourages everyone who is pulled over to remain silent to protest the racial prejudice that motivates such questions. Together, ten unions and civil rights groups sued the State of Georgia on the grounds that this law is unconstitutional.[lviii]

Economists and other pro-immigration groups also argue that this law has had, and will continue to have, disastrous consequences on several industries. Over 900,000 illegal immigrants live in Georgia. They, along with 14,000 foreign students, are affected by this law. Illegal immigrants make up almost 10% of Georgia's population and almost 13% of the state's workforce. If all illegal immigrants were to be removed from Georgia, it would be hit by $21.3 billion in economic losses, $9.5 billion in state GDP loss, and over 132,000 job losses in Georgia's citizen population.[lix]

But the numbers given by economists are tentative. They reflect what could possibly happen if illegal immigrants were removed. There is substantial evidence that shows the negative impact that this law has already had on Georgia's economy. Georgia is famous for its peaches. Unfortunately, because of this law, its farming industry is in shambles. All farmers, whether they use undocumented worker labor or not, suffered over $391 million in losses. Thousands of acres of onions, cotton, and melon were left to rot in Georgia, simply because there was not enough labor to harvest these crops. To alleviate their labor troubles, some anti-immigration groups have been advocating the use of machines to replace workers. However, the switch would cost each farm $1.2 million in farming equipment and lost income due to poorer quality of harvested crops.[ix] Pro-immigration groups use the fact that Georgia has suffered tremendous losses to show that illegal immigration is an integral part of the American economy.

Part II: Immigration – Against

Chapter 1: Groups that Against Immigration

Anti-Immigration sentiment is not an ahistorical phenomenon. Ever since the establishment of the United States, groups have held strong stances either for or against immigration. In 1798, only a few years after the United States won its independence from England, the Alien Enemies was enacted. This act allowed the president to arrest and deport immigrants "if their home countries were at war with the United States." This act has never been repealed.

As the United States got more heavily industrialized, and as demand for cheap labor began growing, nativists and labor unions began campaigning for stricter immigration laws as early as the 1890s. These sentiments and rulings continue to define how groups feel about immigration. Nativists are concerned with maintaining the sanctity of United States citizenship. They favor established residents over immigrants and foreigners.

In 1907, the Dillingham Commission was established for the purpose of documenting and studying immigration patterns to the United States, and its effects. Several nativist groups used the findings of the Dillingham Commission to advocate for stricter controls on immigration. Nativists teamed up with unions in the 1920s because they both had a common fear of low-skilled immigrants flooding the labor market.

Contemporary immigration reductionists believe in either reducing the immigration quota, or enforcing stricter laws against illegal immigration. Most immigration reductionists are more concerned with illegal immigration, as they recognize some of the advantages of having legal, educated immigrants in the United States. Most anti-immigration groups believe that having a high number of immigrants discourages assimilation into American culture. Because immigrants settle in clusters close to members of their own ethnicity, they argue, immigrants are discouraged from learning English. These groups further argue that having too many immigrants can have negative economic and environmental consequences on the country while contributing to high crime rates, urban sprawl, and inner-city decay.

Although there are several anti-immigration groups, this guide will discuss three of the bigger ones:

The American Immigration Control Foundation

This organization was established in Monterey, Virginia in 1983. Although groups like the Southern Poverty Law Center criticize AICF for being white supremacists and dumping all of the nation's social problems on immigrants,[lxi] AICF claims to be "an American non-partisan grassroots activist organization" with "citizens of all races, creeds, and colors." This group advocates securing America's borders from terrorists, drug smugglers, and illegal aliens, and "using maximum manpower" to do so. AICF urges existing legal immigrants to assimilate as soon as they can, and advocates reducing the legal immigration quota so that immigrants can assimilate easily without the crutch of settling with large groups of fellow immigrants from the same country. They are strongly anti-illegal immigration, and seek to deport all illegal immigrants that live in the United States. They also advocate passing stricter regulations and enforcing current laws to penalize "those who knowingly transport, recruit, solicit, or hire illegal aliens." They are also against admitting refugees and guest workers into the United States, arguing that it would only encourage similar amnesty petitions to be filed.[lxii]

Federation for American Immigration Reform

The Federation for American Immigration Reform (FAIR) was founded in 1979. It is the best established anti-immigration group in the United States. FAIR is a national organization that serves as a nonprofit, public-interest group that seeks to change and adjust the immigration policy to better serve and protect national interests. FAIR activities include conducting research, educating the public about the consequences of immigration, media outreach, grassroots organizing, government relations, and litigation and advocacy at the national, state, and local levels. Critics of FAIR have argued that FAIR has received over $1.2 million in aid from the Pioneer Fund to better study links between race and intelligence, making FAIR a racist organization. Representatives from FAIR argue that they have severed all ties to the Pioneer Fund, and say that they seek only to promote a temporary freeze on all immigration except spouses and minor children of U.S citizens and a limited number of refugees. This cessation would allow the government to plan and think of an immigration reform strategy. FAIR calls for a drastic reduction in the immigration quota so that immigration levels are consistent and manageable. The ideal quota, they argue, is 300,000 people a year. In FAIR's view, a successful immigration policy is one that would allow the United States to regain control of its borders and help maintain consistent immigration trends. Officials at FAIR claim that polls show an overwhelming support of this policy. FAIR encourages using laws and technology to end illegal immigration. They also seek to bring legal immigration as low as possible. They seek to discourage immigration by increasing public awareness about the harms of immigration and researching the causes and effects of immigration by sharing research with the public and with leaders in academia, the government, and media. FAIR also engages in various public policy lobbying. FAIR officials also testify on immigration bill cases more than any other immigration organization's officials due to their keen understanding about latest immigration trends and developments. They examine these trends so that immigration policies can be used to best serve environmental, societal and economic interests for all Americans.[lxiii]

FAIR believes that population stabilization would encourage economic development and the alleviation of poverty in immigrant communities. They also argue that bringing in high-skilled immigrant workers creates "brain drains" in their homelands. They argue that having too large of an immigration quota causes a wide variety of social problems, including racial tension, the spread of diseases, and increases in poverty and crime. Unless the United States seals its borders, they argue, the American society will be overrun by people creating garbage and looking for jobs, homes, and education for their children. Research published by FAIR is utilized by academics and government officials to write legislation.[lxiv]

NumbersUSA

This organization provides a civil forum for ethnically and politically diverse Americans to focus their energy on a single issue: the number of people who immigrate to the United States annually. They are concerned with educating the public about the negative consequences of immigration. They also break down immigration legislation to policy makers and government officials by highlighting favorable and unfavorable consequences of a particular law or bill on the table. They favor a decrease in immigration number down to "traditional" levels. They seek to stabilize the American population and run the country with fiscal responsibility, environmental sustainability, fairness in the workplace, and individual freedom and mobility.

A million participants over 435 congressional districts make NumbersUSA the nation's biggest immigration-reduction organization in United States. They're based in Washington D.C and members persuade federal government officials to support immigration policies to protect vulnerable Americans from excessive taxes, loss of wages, and a diminished quality of life while also advocating policies that help the government reduce excessive expenses related to immigration.

NumbersUSA originated in 1996. The firm was founded and led by Roy Beck, a journalist who graduated at the University of Missouri. Beck's career in journalism included reporting from more than 30 states and a dozen countries. He founded the NumbersUSA movement in response to the incredibly high number of immigrants that enter the United States annually. He suggests that the United States adopt the policy which NumbersUSA advocates. His immigration policy centers on choosing the right amount of immigrants who are allowed to enter United States each year. This number is supposed reflect the best interests of American citizens. The policy also depends on regulating illegal entry into the United States.

The main points of his policy include:

1. Cutting the amount of people legally allowed to enter the United States to half a million.
2. Reducing the population so that the quality of life and the state of the environment remains stable for future generations. This part of the policy includes making deep cuts in government spending.
3. Reducing the number of visas that are awarded to extended family members of American citizens.
4. Reducing the number of employment visas and visas given away through the visa lottery system. Beck promotes giving away only temporary guest worker visas, and that too, only in the case of labor shortages. The guest worker visas that he advocates using are much more inflexible than the worker visas in place today.
5. Eliminating birthright citizenship for births to both legal and illegal visitors by collaborating with immigrants' origin countries.
6. Mandating electronic verification systems that would effectively deny jobs and taxpayer-provided benefits to illegal immigrants.
7. Implementing a computerized entry and exit system to monitor visitors who have violated their visas.

8. Promoting immigration only for nuclear family members (including only spouses and minor children, including adopted children), internationally recognized special-needs refugees and immigrants with truly extraordinary skills.

Chapter 2: Arguments Against

Illegal Immigration

Under the following three circumstances, people are considered to be illegal immigrants by the United States government:[lxv]

1. Entry without authorization or inspection.
2. Staying beyond the authorized period after entering legally.
3. Violation of the terms of legal entry (either as Non-immigrant Visa over stayer or Border crossing card violator)

The number of immigrants who have entered illegally without inspection or by evading the Immigration Inspectors and Border Patrol Authorities is 6 to 7 million. There are anywhere from 250,000 to 500,000 border crossing card violators and about 4 to 5.5 million nonimmigrant Visa Overstayers in the United States. In total, these two add up to about 4.5 to 6 million illegal immigrants who entered the United States through legal means. Just under half of all illegal immigrants enter legally. The rest enter through illegal means.[lxvi]

It is usually a lot safer to enter the United States legally and become illegal by either staying beyond the authorized period, or by violating the terms of legal entry. It is much, much more dangerous to enter the United States without authorization or inspection. Besides the fact that armed police may stop entry by force, the actual journey across the border is incredibly dangerous. It spans both the Chihuahuan and the Sonoran deserts. For that reason, it is a common practice for illegal immigrants to hire professional smugglers called "*Coyotes*" to help cross the border. *Coyotes* have a good deal of knowledge about safety issues when crossing the border. They do a risky job and are therefore highly paid. Crossing the border without the use of a *Coyote* is risky, as it can lead to capture or death.

There are three main reasons there are so many illegal immigrants in the United States:[lxvii]
    1. Global economic change (in particular, the increasing globalization of economies).
    2. The inadequacy of channels for legal economic migration.
    3. Ineffective employer sanctions.
The first reason, globalization, is a result of increased international production, distribution, and consumption of goods and labor. Better and faster modes of transportation have allowed information, goods, and labor to be supplied exactly where they are demanded. The global food industry, for example, relies heavily on better and faster transportation, not only to supply the goods where they are needed, but labor and information, as well. Countries are encouraged both by international law and by economic incentives to keep their borders open to

outside investment. It is simply more economically efficient to have a large base of unskilled workers to drive down the minimum wage; competition for jobs is created, and excess labor allows employers to marginalize workers to sell their goods more cheaply, and make more profits themselves. As developed countries shift towards more service-based economies (which require a lot of knowledge and specialization of skills), there has been a shortage of cheap labor. In the United States, for example, the average worker is much more educated than they were fifty years ago. As a result, to supply the labor where it is needed, the movement of labor has also become more international.

This brings us to the second reason of increased illegal migration: The inadequacy of channels for legal economic migration. Regardless of restrictions, there is a demand for cheap labor in the United States, and a supply for it in Mexico, the Honduras, and other nations to the south. Because there is a quota on how many immigrants are let into the United States, legal migration is inadequate; not enough people are coming in legally. Most immigrants come to the United States through their family members. There is an overall limit of 675,000 on legal immigrants each year (not including spouses, children, and parents of citizens). There are only 140,000 visas given to immigrants for job-related reasons. Unfortunately, the immigration system does not give preference to low-skilled workers.[lxviii] Most of the workers who come to the United States legally are high-skilled, and often hold Ph.D.'s. In fact, 40% of Ph.D. holders in United

States are immigrants.[lxix] Immigration channels also inadequate for another reason: The process that lets migrants in takes too long to go through, especially if no family members are citizens.

The third and final reason, ineffective employer sanctions, is the one most targeted by groups who are anti-illegal immigration. It is easy for illegal immigrants to find jobs in the United States simply because not enough regulation is dedicated to stopping their hire. There are three reasons for this ineffectiveness. All three of these reasons are targeted by anti-immigration groups:[lxx]

1.   An absence of reliable mechanisms for verifying employment eligibility.

2.   Inadequate funding of interior immigration enforcement. Exterior immigration enforcement occurs before immigrants enter the country. After they enter the United States, immigration is regulated with interior immigration enforcement. For example, if a person overstays their legal visiting visa, interior immigration enforcement is in charge of sending them back to their country.

3.   An absence of political will to regulate illegal immigration. Political will is not lacking in the United States; rather, it is not strong enough to motivate actions stronger than those that are already put in place. While some feel sympathetic towards illegal immigrants, and believe in being more lenient with them, others lack the political will to deport them from the country simply because they realize that the economic system in the United States requires cheap immigrant labor. There are also those that lack the

political will to regulate illegal immigrants because they believe that the number of illegal immigrants in this country is decreasing. There are several reasons for this decrease: Firstly, border control has become much stronger. Secondly, immigration laws have become tougher. Thirdly, there is a decreased demand in the United States since 2008 for cheap immigrant labor because of the economic crisis. Finally, there are fewer "push" factors out of Hispanic countries: Their economies are healthier, the population is more educated that it once was, and birth rates are lower.[lxxi]

The Border – Why groups want to make it stronger

There is a good reason why most illegal entries to the United States use *coyotes* to enter. There are several dangers associated with crossing the United States and Mexico border. Because of the recent strengthening measures taken to reduce the flux of illegal migrants, illegal immigrants coming from the Southern border of the United States have had to cross over at specific points. These locations are especially dangerous to cross. Operation Gatekeeper, for example, has specifically strengthened the border to the south of San Diego, California, forcing people to travel across the more dangerous Chihuahuan desert to the south of Texas to get to the United States. Those crossing the border are in danger of starving, dying of thirst, heat stroke, and falling prey to wild animals, especially snakes. Some immigrants are killed as they ride on roofs of cargo trains while the trains go through tunnels. Sometimes, when the journey gets too rough, their Coyotes steal whatever meager belongings crossers possess and abandon them in the desert, leaving them exposed to all of the dangers mentioned previously. Besides natural dangers, illegal immigrants are faced with danger when they resist arrest at the border. According to Roberto Martinez, the Director of the U.S. and Mexico Border Program, 418 illegal immigrants died over a period of four years while trying to cross the Mexican border into California from resisting arrest.[lxxii] But illegal immigrants are not the only ones suffering from inadequate border patrolling. In 2008, there were 987 assaults on Border Patrol Agents. Twelve of these assaults resulted in death for the illegal immigrant, as the Patrol Agents shot them in self-defense.

As a result of these circumstances, those people who are against illegal immigration strongly advocate securing the border against illegal immigrants. After the September 11 attacks, public opinion against immigration got stronger, especially when it was discovered that terrorists orchestrating the attacks were illegal immigrants. In fact, out of the ninety-four immigrant terrorists operating between 1990 and 2004 in the United States, almost two-thirds had committed immigration fraud prior to taking part in terrorist activity.[lxxiii] In response to this increased public opposition to illegal immigration, President George W. Bush deployed the National Guard to strengthen the Mexican border. More than six thousand National Guard members had been sent patrol the border by January 2007. This measure cost the United States $750 million.

Things have not changed much under the Obama administration. Border policing has doubled during Obama's presidency, and an average of 400,000 illegal immigrants are deported each year. Nearly $18 billion a year are spent on immigration enforcement. This budget is higher than the budgets of all other federal law enforcement agencies combined, including the FBI and the Secret Service.[lxxiv]

The Economic Consequences of Immigration

The economic effects of immigration is a hotly debated topic. Most illegal (and, to a lesser degree, legal) immigrants come to the United States for economic reasons. Because employer sanctions are not as strictly enforced, it is easier for employers to hire illegal immigrants. Because of this fact, and the fact that illegal immigrants can make more money than they do in their home countries, immigration is attractive. According to a study done by Barry Chiswick, a contributor to the Journal of Economic Perspectives, a group of illegal Mexican immigrants made six times as much money picking fruits and vegetables in Oregon as they did in Mexico. After

Chiswick took the higher cost of living in the United States and the expenses related to traveling to Oregon into account, his study still showed that illegal immigrants were making three times as much as they did doing the same work in Mexico.[lxxv]

Opponents to immigration argue that the incredible influx of immigrants to the United States (2.5 million entries per year) drives up demands for housing. A higher demand for homes and a fixed amount of homes drives up the price of homes. This factor helps explain why homes in crowded urban centers like Los Angeles and New York (both places where immigrant concentration is high, 41% and 36%, respectively) are more expensive than the national average home. Opponents further argue that Hispanic immigrants were responsible for the mortgage crisis of 2008. Because the number of Hispanic immigrants increased from 6 million to 9.2 million from 1990 to 2006,[lxxvi] the banking industry saw their increasing numbers (even illegal immigrants') as an untapped market for home-owner loans. There was a disproportionate number of home foreclosures in Hispanic neighborhoods.[lxxvii]

One of the most common arguments that anti-immigration groups give when advocating reducing the number of immigrants to the country is the fact that high levels of immigration may push down the average wage. If there is always a surplus of workers, as there is when immigration is high, labor unions have more trouble fighting for higher wages. Recent immigrants tend to be poorer than their colleagues, and are not as willing to join labor unions to fight for higher wages. Furthermore, workers, especially those who join unions, are constantly under threat to be replaced by immigrant workers who are willing to work for lower wages. Opponents to immigration argue that paying immigrant workers low wages not only reduces the bargaining power of unions, it also "leads you to a society where a small number are very, very rich, there's nobody in the middle, and everyone is left scrambling for crumbs at the bottom," according to Kenneth Jost, Supreme Court Editor and Professor of Law at Georgetown University.[lxxviii] A similar argument was made by George Borjas, an economist at Harvard University. By creating a competition for wages, immigrants drive down wages and widen the income gap between employers and employees.[lxxix] Borjas further showed in studies that immigration (both legal and illegal) from Mexico and other Central American countries accounted for a 3.7% wage loss for American workers on average, a 4.5% wage loss for African Americans, and a 5% wage loss for non-immigrant Hispanic Americans, and 7.4% for workers who did not have a high school diploma. This study was undertaken using data from 1980 to 2000.[lxxx] When more recent data (1990 to 2004) was analyzed by Economist Giovanni Peri, data showed that the wage was still depressed by immigration by 4%.[lxxxi] According to studies done by the Public Policy Institute of California, hiring illegal immigrants displaces citizens from work and increases crime rates among citizens.[lxxxii]

Another common argument against immigration is the fact that immigrants strain public services, in particular, health and public school services. Thirty-one percent of adult immigrants do not have high school diplomas. Roughly one-third do not have health insurance, and are often cited as slowing down emergency room services. Teachers have to spend extra time with Hispanic children who do not speak English, and they are often put in English-Language Learner classes, which take a larger budget.[lxxxiii]

Illegal Immigrant Children

Many anti-illegal immigration groups express outrage at the fact their valuable tax dollars are going to work to support illegal immigrants. They argue that illegal immigrants do not pay taxes regularly. They further argue that the strain they put on public service system is more costly than whatever benefits they might be bringing into the country. Illegal immigrant children put just as much strain as adults into public systems that taxpayers put a lot of wealth into building up. Seven percent of all school children (1.8 million total) are estimated to be illegal immigrants. Estimates of the nation-wide costs associated with educating these children (in 2009) range from $11.2 billion a year to $30 billion a year.[lxxxiv lxxxv] Not only are there education costs associated with putting illegal immigrant children through a K-12 school system, some states, like the state of California, reduces tuition for illegal immigrants who have attended high school in the state for three years or more. These reductions are possible because government funding from taxes offsets part of the fees associated with attending school. Furthermore, the majority of illegal immigrant school children do not even graduate high school. On average, they only make it to the tenth grade. One of the reasons for this fact is that these children have more pressure and stress to work at a younger age to supplement the less-than-minimum wage their parents may be making. They also do not have the economic resources to continue on with higher education, so they do not see the point in getting a high school diploma.[lxxxvi] Opponents to immigration argue that immigrant children pose a cost that is too high on our services. Besides the costs associated with education, there are various costs associated with providing social services to illegal immigrants and their children. In Alabama, for example, expenditure on illegal immigrant education and social services amounts to about $250 million.[lxxxvii]

One of the most hotly debated issue among pro- and anti-immigration groups is the fact that children born in the United States are granted citizenship, regardless of their parents' immigration status. Many pregnant women cross the Mexican border to have "anchor babies." Almost all immigration groups want the law that allows "anchor babies" to be repealed. They argue that this law motivates non-Americans to migrate illegally, as most social workers are unwilling to separate newborn babies from their mothers (in cases of deportation). Many questions arise from the practice of having children in the United States to "anchor" parents here. Can nursing mothers be deported if their children are American citizens? Can such families be separated? American citizens cannot be deported in the absence of extreme criminal activity. Anti-immigration groups advocate either repealing the law that allows "anchor babies" or reforming it so that these questions can be answered. Ira Mehlman, a spokesman for FAIR, argued that illegal immigrants should be deported whether they have children or not. "Children are not human shields. Nobody wants to hurt anybody's kids. But any time parents break the law, it has an impact on the children."[lxxxviii] The problem of anchor babies is not a small one; nearly 10% (340,000 total) of all children born in the United States are children of illegal immigrants. There are 11.2 million illegal immigrants living in the United States. These immigrants have 4.5 million American citizen children between them. These children, although technically Americans, fare just as poorly in school as illegal immigrant children.[lxxxix]

Environment

Anti-immigration groups often argue that having a bigger influx of immigrants is detrimental to the environment, as population increases due to high rates of immigration puts stress on natural resources like groundwater supplies. According to statistics provided by California Department of Water

Resources if more water supplies are not found by the year 2020, California residents will inevitably face a water shortage more severe than any that has ever been experience before. The population growth rate due to births is already quite high in California. Additionally, about half a million people migrate to California every year. If it continues to rise at this rate, by the year 2030, the population will have reached forty-eight million people. Since Southern California is a coastal desert, it is only able to supply water to fulfill the needs of one million people on its own. Water stress in Northern California is growing. Aqueducts are running more water than ever to satisfy the thirst of an ever-growing population. The environmental consequences associated with the construction and use of such aqueducts is enormous.[xc]

Besides putting a strain on water supplies, rising waves of border-hoppers are causing heavy damage to the lands located near the Mexican border. At some places, the impacts of immigration on the land are found to be extremely shocking. Mike Coffeen, a biologist with the Fish and Wildlife Service in Tucson, Arizona says that environmental degradation has become a visible consequence of large-scale illegal immigration. His group found 45 abandoned cars at Buenos Aires near Sasabe, Arizona, and enough trash to fill 723 large trash bags. (That's about 18,000 pounds of garbage.[xci] Garbage is not only unsightly; it can be dangerous. Illegal Immigrants were suspected of causing at least eight major wildfires in Arizona the year 2002 alone. The fires spread over an area of 68,413 acres and cost taxpayers approximately $5.1 million in repairs.[xcii]

Criminal Activity among Illegal Immigrants

Although the effects of immigration on the economy are not as well-documented (arguments go both way, for whether immigration is good or bad for the economy), the effects of immigration on crime are obvious and easy to understand. Legal immigration seems not to have as much effect on crime while illegal immigration does. According to data collected by the Department of Homeland Security, 240,000 illegal immigrants have been convicted of crimes *unrelated* to immigration in 2010. Thirty thousand of these cases have resulted in deportation.[xciii] In 1999, putting criminals through law enforcement systems (for crimes unrelated to immigration) cost California, Arizona, New Mexico, and Texas over $108 million. In San Diego alone, these costs represent 9% of the county's total budget.[xciv] Illegal immigrants made up almost 15% of Arizona's prison population in 2010, even though they represent less than 7% of Arizona's total population. And illegal immigrants do not just commit petty crimes; according to the Arizona Department of Corrections, in 2010, illegal immigrants represented 40% of criminals incarcerated for kidnapping, 24% of those incarcerated for dealing drugs, and 13% of murderers[xcv]. Arizona is not a mere case study; criminal activity is highest in illegal immigrants as a community. In Los Angeles, for example, illegal immigrants represent 95% of those arrested for homicide and 67% of those arrested for fugitive felons. Sixty percent of all gang members in Southern California were also said to be illegal immigrants in 1995.[xcvi]

One of the most common crimes that illegal immigrants are charged with committing is identity theft. Those who have their identities stolen express outrage because other crimes like tax evasion begin to be associated with their persona. Illegal immigrants often use social security numbers so they can work at or above minimum wage. They also use social security numbers to get services from the government, like sending their children to school, getting medical care under Medical, and receiving unemployment benefits. Some particularly skilled illegal immigrants can use identity theft to obtain baking information and commit credit card fraud. According to the US Supreme Court's ruling in *Flores-Figueroa v. United States*, however, illegal immigrants cannot be prosecuted if they were not aware that the numbers belonged to someone. To be prosecuted, they must be aware that they were stealing someone's identity.

Getting your identity stolen is not the most dangerous way illegal immigrants can hurt you, anti-immigration groups argue. By sending illegal immigrants to the United States, large drug-cartels push their control and expand their territory outwards into the United States. Then, their agents can receive and distribute drugs from Mexico to Americans. Drugs are even shipped via illegal immigrants because small masses can be worth incredible sums of money. Sometimes, drugs are stored in condoms and swallowed by illegal immigrants called "drug mules." They are contained within border crossers' internal organs and are defecated, opened up, and sold.[xcvii] After their delivery, drug mules continue to live in the United States, sometimes cultivating marijuana within National forests while perpetuating the control that a drug lord has over a territory.[xcviii]

The previous section, "The Border" talked about how the public responded defensively to terrorist attacks. After September 11, 2001, the threat of terrorist activities in the United States got stronger. The government's and the public's fears were not unfounded. Almost two-thirds of all terrorist activities are undertaken by illegal immigrants. Even some those who are legal immigrants at the time of their crimes have had illegal immigration in their records. For example, some terrorists had overstayed their visas previously, applied for asylum under false pretenses, and faked marriages to win residency and avoid deportation.[xcix]

Illegal immigrants are not the only ones who have higher-than-average crime rates. Although immigrants themselves are unlikely to be arrested, the children of immigrants are more likely than their peers to be arrested and incarcerated. One of the reasons this fact may be is that immigrants often settle in poorer neighborhoods, where crime rates are already high.[c]

Chapter 3: Important Legal Cases and Legislation

USA Patriot Act

One act of legislation that was enacted in response to higher levels of terrorist activity was the USA Patriot Act. This act gave the government surveillance rights over residents and citizens, and it expanded significantly the conditions which would allow deportation of suspicious individuals. Under this act, suspects would not have to engage in any terrorist activity to warrant a deportation; their affiliation with any terrorist or anarchist group was enough to warrant arrest and deportation. To label an organization as threatening to either the Attorney General or the Secretary of State had to simply signify it as such. After this labeling, any individuals found affiliating with the labeled organizations is "certified." This means that the government is labeling the people in question as dangerous to national security. After certification, individuals are jailed indefinitely. There is no opportunity for a hearing or a trial. This act has been highly criticized by humanitarian groups, immigration groups, and ethnicity-based groups because it violates the Fifth Amendment of the Constitution, which grants all criminals due process of law. In response to criticisms, the federal government has cited Kwong Hai Chew c. Colding (1953), saying, "The Bill of Rights is a futile authority for the alien seeking admission for the first time to these shores. But once an alien lawfully enters and resides in this country he becomes invested with the rights guaranteed by the Constitution to all people within our borders". In other words, by coming illegally to a country, immigrants give up all of their rights. None of the rights guaranteed by the Constitution or lesser documents apply. Humanitarian groups expressed outrage at this ruling, but the government uses it to this day to detain any illegal immigrant they see fit with no rights promised.

IRIRA

IRIRA (The Illegal Immigration Reform and Immigrant Responsibility Act of 1996) is another law which penalized illegal immigration greatly. Before this law was passed, illegal immigration was penalized by deportation only for criminal offenses, which would warrant five years or more in jail. IRIRA, however, states that illegal immigrants who stay in the United States for 180 to 365 days must stay outside the United States for three or more years. If they stay in the United States for more than 365 days, they must stay outside the United States for at least ten years before attempting to re-enter legally. In both cases, some illegal immigrants may be pardoned and can come to the United States sooner. If they attempt to re-enter before their time outside is up, they cannot apply for waivers for a period of ten years. While this law may sound complicated, the main thing to understand in regards to IRIRA is the fact that immigrants could now be deported for petty criminal offenses. Minor criminal acts like shoplifting and traffic violations make immigrants eligible for deportation. From 1996 to 2001, this law was also applied to any and all illegal immigrants that had violated a minor law or committed a petty crime before 1996. In 2001, however, the Supreme Court ruled in INS v. St. Cyr that applying this law retroactively to those who plead guilty was not constitutional.

Nevertheless, the amount of deportations skyrocketed. Although deportations in the early 1990s were averaging 40,000 illegal immigrants per year, after 1996, after IRIRA was passed, this number increased dramatically. Between the years 1996 and 2005, the average increase to 180,000 people. Less than half of those deported were being deported under criminal grounds. Rather, they were deported simply because they had immigrated illegally.

In 2010, under the Obama Administration, 396,906 people were deported. Out of those, 180,208 had committed no crimes, minor or major. However, almost 50,000 deportations were for "drug-related" crimes, and over 1,000 were for homicide convicts.[ci]

Catching illegal immigrants for deportation is not so easy, though. Some cities are "sanctuary cities," which means that police and other law enforcement officials are not allowed to ask whether a person is legally in the United States or not. Sanctuary may not be given by law, but by habit, as police are encouraged informally to leave questions of legal status alone. Sanctuary cities generally do not allow their funds to be used to catch illegal immigrants. They also discourage employers from asking about legal status. The reason sanctuary cities exist is because law enforcement agents are required to keep the good faith of everyone in their community. If cities begin deporting every illegal immigrant who commits a petty crime, cooperation with law enforcers can take a big hit.

Anti-immigration groups are strictly against having sanctuary cities. This is because they believe that sanctuary policies have caused problems with crime by illegal immigrants since police cannot report them for deportation. They are not motivated to stop committing crimes, because no matter what they do, they are protected from being kicked out [cii]. They further argue that sanctuary policies are against the spirit of IRIRA, as it prevents criminals from being deported.

The Arizona Senate Bill 1070

This law (also known as "Support Our Law Enforcement and Safe Neighborhoods Act) is one of the strictest immigration laws in history. This law made it a misdemeanor for immigrants to live and be in Arizona without having their documents on them at all times. Police officers also are *required* to ask any person during any stop, arrest, or contact about their legal status, even if the police officer does not suspect that the person is an illegal immigrant. This law uses the fact that all non-citizens are required by the United States federal government to register and keep their registration documents on their person at all times. The federal law, however, is not as strictly enforced. Proponents of the Arizona State law argue that it simply enforces the federal law. Besides requiring law enforces to directly police the legal status of the community, the Arizona Senate Bill 1070 also penalizes those who shelter, hire, and transport immigrants travelling without their documentation. This portion of the law, anti-immigration groups argue, was extremely necessary to prevent the economic consequences associated with hiring illegal immigrants. Furthermore, when police or other law enforcement agents fail to enforce this law, Arizona citizens have the right to sue them.

There are many reasons why this strict law came into being. Firstly, Arizona has had a lot of trouble with illegal immigrants. Because it is so close to the border, many illegal immigrants cross the border and settle in Arizona. In fact, Arizona has the largest number of illegal immigrant crossings. In 2010, there were 460,000 estimated illegal immigrants in Arizona, more than five times as many from 1990 levels[ciii]. The large influx of illegal immigrants was not the only concern for the Arizona Senate; criminal activity by illegal immigrants had also become increasingly problematic. By 2009, there was an average of one kidnapping per *day* in Phoenix, Arizona. These statistics are higher than those of any other city in the whole world. Arizona citizens were concerned that the high number of kidnappings were occurring as a result of some spillover warfare from the Mexican Drug War[civ]. There was also concern among Arizona public that increasing illegal immigration was having a negative effect on the economy, especially after the recession of 2008[cv].

The final straw was the killing of Robert Krentz and his dog, an Arizona citizen who was fixing his fence on his ranch. His property was nineteen miles away from the border. Arizona police suspected illegal immigrants for the shooting, since footprints were traced from Krentz's ranch to the Mexican border. This killing increased public and senate support for the Arizona bill.[cvi]

This law was not passed without criticism. Critics claimed that this law would encourage law enforcers to engage in racist behavior, as the vast majority of Arizona's illegal immigrant population is of Hispanic origin. To address this criticism, the bill was changed so that law enforcers would not be allowed to racially profile the people that they stop; rather, they had to indiscriminately ask for papers to all who they stop or engage with[cvii].

[i] Jeane Batalova and Aaron Terrezas. December 2010. "Frequently Requested Statistics on Immigrants and Immigration in the United States." Migration Information Source. Accessed online at <http://www.migrationinformation.org/feature/display.cfm?ID=818>

[ii] [Lymari Morales. 5 August 2009. "Americans Return to Tougher Immigration Stance." Gallup. Accessed online at http://www.gallup.com/poll/122057/americans-return-tougher-immigration-stance.aspx>

[iii] Rita James Simon and Mohamed Alaa Abdel-Moneim, Public opinion in the United States: studies of race, religion, gender, and issues that matter (2010) pp 61–2

[iv] Hiroshi Motomura. 17 December 2007. Americans in Waiting: The Lost Story of Immigration and Citizenship in the United States.

[v] Peter Wallsten (17 Nov 2012). "New super PAC hopes to give cover to pro-immigration Republicans". Washington Post. Accessed Online at http://www.washingtonpost.com/politics/new-super-pac-hopes-to-give-cover-to-pro-immigration-republicans/2012/11/16/c3070b74-300b-11e2-a30e-5ca76eeec857_story.html

[vi] J.D. Harrison. 11 February 2013. "Lawmakers, entrepreneurs, push immigration proposals ahead of State of the Union." The Washington Post. Accessed

online at <http://articles.washingtonpost.com/2013-02-11/business/37047642_1_immigration-reform-immigration-laws-foreign-born-entrepreneurs>

[vii] ibid., J.D Harrison

[viii] Elizabeth Dwoskin. 31 January 2013. "Six Reasons Immigration Reform Has a Good Shot This Year." Bloomberg Businessweek. Accessed Online at <http://www.businessweek.com/articles/2013-01-31/6-reasons-immigration-reform-has-a-good-shot-this-year>

[ix] Raquel Rubio-Goldsmith, M. Melissa McCormick, Daniel Martinez, Inez Magdalena Duarte (2006-10). "The "Funnel Effect" & Recovered Bodies of Unauthorised Migrants Processed by the Pima County Office of the Medical Examiner, 1990-2005." Binational Migration Institute. Mexican American Studies & Research Center at the University of Arizona.

[x] Raquel Rubio-Goldsmith, M. Melissa McCormick, Daniel Martinez and Inez Magdalena Duarte. February 2007 "A Humanitarian Crisis at the Border: New Estimates of Deaths Among Unauthorized Immigrants." Immigration Policy Center. Accessed online at <http://www.americanimmigrationcouncil.org/sites/default/files/docs/Crisis%20at%20the%20Border.pdf>

[xi] ["About Us." National Council of La Raza. Accessed Online at <http://www.nclr.org/index.php/about_us/>

[xii] ["About Us." National Council of La Raza. Accessed Online at <http://www.nclr.org/index.php/about_us/>].

[xiii] Davidson, Adam (30 March 2006). "Q&A: Illegal Immigrants and the U.S. Economy". National Public Radio. Accessed online at <http://www.npr.org/templates/story/story.php?storyId=5312900>

[xiv] Julian Simon. 1989. "The Economic Consequences of Immigration." Cato Group Policy. Accessed online at <http://www.cato.org/pubs/policy_report/pr-imopi.html>

[xv] Statistics on U.S. Immigration: An Assessment of Data Needs for Future Research. (1997) Committee on National Statistics and Committee on Population. National Research Council. Page 6

[xvi] Hanson, Gordon H.; Raymond Robertson, and Antonio Spilimbergo (2002). "Does Border Enforcement Protect U.S. Workers from Illegal Immigration?". *The Review of Economics and Statistics* **84** (1): 73–92.

[xvii] Perez, Miguel. 22 August 2006. "Hire education: Immigrants aren't taking jobs from Americans." Chicago Sun-Times. Accessed Online at <http://www.highbeam.com/doc/1P2-1633663.html>

[xviii] Lowenstein, Roger. 9 July 2006. "The Immigration Equation." The New York Times. Accessed online at <http://www.nytimes.com/2006/07/09/magazine/09IMM.html>

[xix] Jason Richwine. August 24, 2009.The Congealing Pot—Today's Immigrants Are Different from Waves Past. National Review. Accessed online at <http://www.aei.org/article/100860>

[xx] About Us. USCIS About Us Page. Accessed online at <http://www.uscis.gov/portal/site/uscis/menuitem.eb1d4c2a3e5b9ac89243c6a7543f6d1a/?vgnextoid=2af29c7755cb9010VgnVCM10000045f3d6a1RCRD&vgnextchannel=2af29c7755cb9010VgnVCM10000045f3d6a1RCRD>

[xxi] Dr. Raul Hinojosa-Ojeda. January 2010. "Raising the Floor for American Workers." Immigration Policy Center. Accessed online at <http://www.immigrationpolicy.org/sites/default/files/docs/Hinojosa%20-%20Raising%20the%20Floor%20for%20American%20Workers%20010710.pdf>

[xxii] ["Immigration's Economic Impact." 20 June 2007. The White House: Council of Economic Advisers. Accessed online at <http://georgewbush-whitehouse.archives.gov/cea/cea_immigration_062007.html>

[xxiii] Survey of Business Owners: Hispanic-Owned Firms." 21 March, 2006. U.S. Department of Commerce. Accessed online at <http://www.census.gov/newsroom/releases/archives/news_conferences/2006-03-21_news_conference.html>

[xxiv] Aaron Terrazas and Jeanne Batalova. Frequently Requested Statistics on Immigrants in the United States. Migration Policy Institute, October 2009. Accessed online at <http://www.migrationinformation.org/feature/display.cfm?ID=818>

[xxv] "Immigration's Economic Impact." 20 June 2007.

The White House: Council of Economic Advisers. Accessed online at <http://georgewbush-whitehouse.archives.gov/cea/cea_immigration_06200 7.html>

xxvi Giovanni Peri. May 2012. "Rationalizing U.S. Immigration Policy: Reforms for Simplicity, Fairness, and Economic Growth." Discussion Paper 2012-01. The Hamilton Project. Accessed online at <http://www.brookings.edu/~/media/research/files/pa pers/2012/5/15%20immigration%20peri/05_immigrat ion_peri_paper.pdf>

xxvii Espenshade, Thomas J. and Belanger, Maryanne (1998) "Immigration and Public Opinion." In Marcelo M. Suarez-Orozco, ed. Crossings: Mexican Immigration in Interdisciplinary Perspectives. Cambridge, Mass.: David Rockefeller Center for Latin American Studies and Harvard University Press, pages 365-403

xxviii Jost, Kenneth. 9 Mar 2012. "Immigration Conflict: Should States Crack down on Unlawful Aliens?" The CQ Researcher Online 22.10 (1923): n. pag. CQ Researcher by CQ Press. Accessed online at <http://library.cqpress.com/cqresearcher/document.ph p?id=cqresrre2012030900>.

xxix ["The State of American Public Opinion on Immigration in Spring 2006: A Review of Major Surveys." 17 May 2006. Pew Hispanic Center. Accessed online at <http://www.pewhispanic.org/files/factsheets/18.pdf>

xxx Backgrounder: Immigrants in the United States, 2007, Center for Immigration Studies, Nov. 2007, p. 31

[xxxi] ["The Role of Immigrants in the U.S. Labor Market." November 2005. The Congress of the United States - Congressional Budget Office. Accessed online at <http://www.cbo.gov/sites/default/files/cbofiles/ftpdocs/68xx/doc6853/11-10-immigration.pdf>

[xxxii] George Borjas. May 2004. "Increasing the Supply of Labor Through Immigration." Center for Immigration Studies. Accessed Online at <http://www.cis.org/articles/2004/back504.html>

[xxxiii] Raul Hinojosa-Ojeda. Spring, 2000. "Labor Market Impacts of Amnesty: A Comparative Analysis of IRCA and current conditions". UCLA North American Integration and Development Center. Accessed online at <http://www.naid.ucla.edu/uploads/4/2/1/9/4219226/b46.pdf>

[xxxiv] J. Lipman, Francine, J. Spring 2006. Taxing Undocumented Immigrants: Separate, Unequal and Without Representation. The Tax Lawyer. Paper number 06-20 Accessed online at <http://papers.ssrn.com/sol3/papers.cfm?abstract_id=881584>

[xxxv] Bianca Vasquez Toness. 5 March 2007. "U.S. Tax Program for Illegal Immigrants Under Fire." National Public Radio. Accessed online at <http://www.npr.org/templates/story/story.php?storyId=7718604>

[xxxvi] Riley, Jason. 15 May, 2008. Let Them In: The Case for Open Borders. Gotham Publishers. New York City, NY. p. 95

[xxxvii] Cato Handbook for Congress. 2003. Cato

Institute, Washington DC. Accessed online at
<http://www.cato.org/sites/cato.org/files/serials/files/
cato-handbook-policymakers/2003/9/hb108-63.pdf>
xxxviii Jim Wilson. 5 April 2005. "Illegal Immigrants
Are Bolstering Social Security With Billions." The
New York Times. Accessed online at
<http://www.nytimes.com/2005/04/05/business/05im
migration.html?_r=0&ei=5090&en=78c87ac4641dc3
83&ex=1270353600&adxnnl=1&pagewanted=2&adx
nnlx=1363198242-dQbt0XZ1WSYfReZPJv5McA>
xxxix Will Dunham. 13 March 2007. "Medicaid
spends 1% on illegal immigrants: study." Reuters.
Accessed online at
<http://www.reuters.com/article/2007/03/13/us-
immigrants-idUSN1346120320070313>
xl Donald J. Hernandez and Evan Charney. 1998.
From Generation to Generation: The Health and
Well-Being of Children in Immigrant Families.
Committee on the Health and Adjustment of
Immigrant Children and Families. National Council
and Institute of Medicine. Accessed online at
<http://www.nap.edu/catalog.php?record_id=6164#to
c>
xli James p. Smith, Chair. The New Americans:
Economic, Demographic, and Fiscal Effects of
Immigration (1997) Commission on Behavioral and
Social Sciences and Education (CBASSE), National
Academy of Sciences. page 5
xlii Kristin F. Butcher and Anne Morrison Piehl.
February 2008. "Crime, Corrections, and California."
California Counts: Population Trends and Profiles.
Volume 9 Number 3. Accessed online at

<http://www.ppic.org/content/pubs/cacounts/CC_2 08KBCC.pdf>

[xliii] Don Barnett. 11 October 2006. "A New Era of Refugee Resettlement." Immigration Daily. Accessed online at <http://www.ilw.com/articles/2007,0129-barnett.shtm#bio>

[xliv] ["Refugees in Japan." 12 October 2008. The Japan Times. Accessed online at <http://www.japantimes.co.jp/opinion/2008/10/12/editorials/refugees-in-japan/#.UUOuM1vwLDY>]

[xlv] Scott Rempell. 8 October 2011. "Defining Persecution." Utah Law Review, Volume 2013. No. 1, 2013. Accessed online at <http://papers.ssrn.com/sol3/papers.cfm?abstract_id=1941006>

[xlvi] Lee, Margaret. 12 May 2006. "U.S. Citizenship of Persons Born in the United States to Alien Parents." Congressional Research Service Report for Congress. Washington DC. UNT Digital Library. pp. 10, 17. Accessed online at <http://digital.library.unt.edu/ark:/67531/metacrs9011/>

[xlvii] Preston, Julia. 17 November, 2007. "Immigration Quandary: A Mother Torn From Her Baby". New York Times.

[xlviii] Julia Preston. 17 November 2007. "Immigration Quandary: A Mother Torn From Her Baby." New York Times. Accessed online at <http://www.nytimes.com/2007/11/17/us/17citizen.html?pagewanted=all&_r=0>

[xlix] ibid., Julia Preston

[l] ibid., Julia Preston

[li] Bill Keller. 3 February 2013. "Selling Amnesty." The New York Times. Accessed online at <http://www.nytimes.com/2013/02/04/opinion/keller-selling-amnesty.html?pagewanted=all>

[lii] Brian Bennett. 2 January 2013. "White House eases path to residency for some illegal immigrants." Los Angeles Times. Accessed online at <http://www.latimes.com/news/politics/la-pn-obama-illegal-immigration-residency-20130102,0,181647.story>

[liii] ibid., Brian Bennett

[liv] Jon Freere. 15 September 2010. "Despite Media Mythmaking, the DREAM Act is for Adults." Center for Immigration Studies. Accessed online at <http://cis.org/feere/dream-act-is-for-adults>

[lv] Allison Sherry. 2 October 2012. "Mitt Romney would honor Obama administration's illegal immigrant work permits." Denver Post. Accessed online at <http://www.denverpost.com/nationalpolitics/ci_21676605/romney-wont-deport-young-illegals-who-have-temporary#ixzz2890s7Irl>

[lvi] Tracy Lopez. 23 August 2012. "Baltimore Welcomes Immigrants - No Questions Asked." Fox News Latino. Accessed online at <http://latino.foxnews.com/latino/lifestyle/2012/08/23/baltimore-welcomes-immigrants-no-questions-asked/>].

[lvii] Jacqueline J. Holness. 06 June 2011. "Georgia Immigration Law Called Unconstitutional 'in its Entirety.'" Courthouse News Service. Accessed online at

<http://www.courthousenews.com/2011/06/06/37103.htm>

[lviii] ibid., Jacqueline J. Holness

[lix] Wendy Sefsaf. 01 March 2011. "Georgia State Legislature Pursuing Budget Busting Solutions to Immigration." Immigration Policy Center. Accessed online at <http://www.immigrationpolicy.org/newsroom/release/georgia-state-legislature-pursuing-budget-busting-solutions-immigration>

[lx] Azadeh Shahshahani. 20 May 2012. "HB 87 Negatively Impacts Georgia Economy and Reputation." HuffPost. Accessed online at <http://www.huffingtonpost.com/azadeh-shahshahani/georgia-immigration-policy_b_1528987.html>

[lxi] "Anti Immigration Groups" Spring 2001. Intelligence Report, Issue Number 101. Southern Poverty Law Center. Accessed Online at <http://www.splcenter.org/get-informed/intelligence-report/browse-all-issues/2001/spring/blood-on-the-border/anti-immigration->

[lxii] "About AIC. Americans for Immigration Control. Accessed Online at <http://www.immigrationcontrol.com/>"]

[lxiii] "About Us." FAIR homepage. Accessed online at <http://www.fairus.org/about>].

[lxiv] "About Us." FAIR homepage. Accessed online at <http://www.fairus.org/about>].

[lxv] Modes of Entry for the Unauthorized Migrant Population." May 22, 2006. Pew Hispanic Center

lxvi ibid., Modes of Entry for the Unauthorized Migrant Population

lxvii Judith Gans. Feb. 2007. "Illegal Immigration to the United States: Causes and Policy Solutions." Udall Center for Studies in Public Policy. Accessed online at <http://udallcenter.arizona.edu/immigration/publicati ons/fact_sheet_no_3_illegal_immigration.pdf>

lxviii Jost, Kenneth. "Immigration Conflict: Should States Crack down on Unlawful Aliens?" The CQ Researcher Online 22.10 (1923): n. pag. CQ Researcher by CQ Press. 9 Mar. 2012. Accessed online at <http://library.cqpress.com/cqresearcher/document.ph p?id=cqresrre2012030900>

lxix William A. Wulf, President, National Academy of Engineering, Speaking before the 109th US Congress, September 15, 2005

lxx ibid., Judith Gans. Feb. 2007.

lxxi Jeffery Passel, D'Vera Cohn, and Ana Gonzales-Barrera. 3 May 2012. "Net Migration from Mexico Falls to Zero -- and Perhaps Less." PewResearch Hispanic Center. Accessed online at <http://www.pewhispanic.org/2012/04/23/net-migration-from-mexico-falls-to-zero-and-perhaps-less/>]

lxxii Roberto Martinez. 1999. "Operation Gatekeeper" InMotionMagazine.com. Accessed online at http://www.inmotionmagazine.com/rm99.html]

lxxiii Janice L. Kephart. September 2005. "Moving Beyond the 9/11 Staff report on Terrorist Travel." Center for Immigration Studies. Acessed online at

<http://www.cis.org/articles/2005/kephart.pdf>

lxxiv Dors Meissner, Donald M. Kerwin, Muzaffar Chishti, and Claire Bergeron. January 2013. "Immigration Enforcement in the United States." Washington DC: Migration Policy Institute. Accessed online at <http://www.migrationpolicy.org/pubs/enforcementpillars.pdf>

lxxv Chiswick, Barry R. "Illegal Immigration and Immigration Control". The Journal of Economic Perspectives. Vol. 2, No. 3 (Summer, 1988), pp. 101-115

lxxvi Rosenzweig, Paul. 25 October 2006. "Importing Poverty: Immigration and Poverty in the United States: A Book of Charts". Heritage.org. Accessed online at <http://www.heritage.org/research/reports/2006/10/importing-poverty-immigration-and-poverty-in-the-united-states-a-book-of-charts>

lxxvii Garcia, Adriana (January 30, 2008). "Immigrants hit hard by slowdown, subprime crisis". Reuters. Accessed online at <http://www.reuters.com/article/2008/01/30/us-usa-economy-immigrants-idUSN3019759720080130?feedType=RSS&feedName=domesticNews&pageNumber=1&virtualBrandChannel=0&sp=true>

lxxviii Jost, Kenneth. 9 Mar. 2012. "Immigration Conflict: Should States Crack down on Unlawful Aliens?" The CQ Researcher Online 22.10 (1923): n. pag. CQ Researcher by CQ Press. Accessed Online at <http://library.cqpress.com/cqresearcher/document.ph

p?id=cqresrre2012030900>

[lxxix] Miller, Debra A."Illegal Immigration"(2007).Reference Point Press. 20-23

[lxxx] George J. Borjas. May 2004."Increasing the Supply of Labor Through Immigration" "Center for Immigration Studies". Cis.org. Accessed Online at <http://www.cis.org/articles/2004/back504.html>].

[lxxxi] Giovanni Peri. February 2007. "How Immigrants Affect California Employment and Wages (PPIC Publication)". Ppic.org

[lxxxii] Kristin F. Butcher and Annie Morrison Piehl. February 2008. "Crime, Corrections, and California". Public Policy Institute of California. Volume 9, Number 3.

[lxxxiii] Haya El Nasser and Kathy Kiely. 12 December 2005. "Study: Immigration grows, reaching record numbers." USA Today. Accessed Online at <http://usatoday30.usatoday.com/news/nation/2005-12-12-immigration_x.htm>

[lxxxiv] The Impact of Unauthorized Immigrants on the Budgets of State and Local Governments," Congressional Budget Office, Dec. 2009, p. 8

[lxxxv] "S&P Study: Costs and Benefits of Undocumented Immigrants," Hispanic News, May 1, 2009, p. 2

[lxxxvi] Teresa Watanabe. 22 October 2011. "Study finds education gap for illegal Mexican migrants' children." Los Angeles Times. Accessed online at <http://articles.latimes.com/2011/oct/22/local/la-me-illegal-academics-20111023>

[lxxxvii] Chip Reid. 23 November 2011. "Consequences of Alabama immigration law set in". CBS News.

Accessed online at <http://www.cbsnews.com/8301-18563_162-57330809/consequences-of-alabama-immigration-law-set-in/>

lxxxviii Julia Preston. 17 November 2007. Immigration Quandary: A Mother Torn from Her Baby. The New York Times. Accessed online at <http://www.nytimes.com/2007/11/17/us/17citizen.html?pagewanted=print>

lxxxix Jeffery Passel and Paul Taylor. August 11, 2010. "Unauthorized Immigrants and Their U.S.-Born Children." Pew Hispanic Center. Accessed Online at <http://www.pewhispanic.org/2010/08/11/unauthorized-immigrants-and-their-us-born-children/>

xc Paul Rogers. 25 April 2012. "State looks to the sea for drinkable water" Contra Costa Times. Accessed online at <http://www.contracostatimes.com/portlet/article/html/fragments/print_article.jsp?articleId=6057081&siteId=571>]

xci Arthur H. Rotstein. 12 July 2004. "Dumping of Trash: Endemic in State with Flood of Illegal Immigration." Associated Press Newswires. Dateline Coronado National Memorial, Arizona]

xcii Illegal Immigrants Tied to Costly Wildfires Associated Press." 9 September 2002. Dateline Tucson, Arizona]

xciii Slevin, Peter. July 26, 2010. "Deportation of illegal immigrants increases under Obama administration". Washington Post. Accessed online at <http://www.washingtonpost.com/wp-dyn/content/article/2010/07/25/AR2010072501790.html>

[xciv] Tanis J. Salant and others, Illegal Immigrants in U.S./Mexico Border Counties: The Costs for Law Enforcement, Criminal Justice, and Emergency Medical Services (report prepared for the United States/Mexico Border Counties Coalition, February 2001)

[xcv] Laura Strickler. July 22, 2010. "Undocumented Immigrants Increasingly Filling Arizona Prisons." CBS News. Accessed online at <http://www.cbsnews.com/8301-31727_162-20011391-10391695.html?tag=contentMain;contentBody>].

[xcvi] Heather Mac Donald (September 5, 2001). "The Illegal-Alien Crime Wave by Heather Mac Donald, City Journal Summer 2004". City-journal.org. Accessed online at <http://www.city-journal.org/html/14_1_the_illegal_alien.html>

[xcvii] House of Representatives, Subcommittee on Immigration and Claims, Committee on the Judiciary, Border Security and Deterring Illegal Entry Into the United States House.gov, April 23, 1997

[xcviii] "Illegal immigrant arrested at marijuana garden on Six Rivers" 2 October 2008. Eureka Times-Standard

[xcix] "Visa Overstays: Can We Bar the Terrorist Door?" 109th Congress Meeting. May 11, 2006. Accessed online at <http://commdocs.house.gov/committees/intlrel/hfa27480.000/hfa27480_0.HTM>

[c] Tony Walters. 1999. *Crime and Immigrant Youth*. Sage Publications

[ci] Jim Barnett (October 18, 2011). "U.S. deportations

reach historic levels". CNN. Accessed online at<http://www.cnn.com/2011/10/18/us/immigrant-deportations/>

[cii] Heather Mac Donald (September 5, 2001). "The Illegal-Alien Crime Wave by Heather Mac Donald, City Journal Summer 2004". City-journal.org. Accessed online at <http://www.city-journal.org/html/14_1_the_illegal_alien.html>].

[ciii] Spagat, Elliot (May 13, 2010). "Other border states shun Arizona's immigration law". Associated Press. MSNBC. Accessed online at <http://www.azcentral.com/news/articles/2010/05/12/20100512immigration-crackdown-border-states-arizona-law.html

[civ] Archibold, Randal C. (June 20, 2010). "On Border Violence, Truth Pales Compared to Ideas".*The New York Times*: p. 18. Accessed online at <http://www.nytimes.com/2010/06/20/us/20crime.html?_r=0>

[cv] [Nowicki, Dan (July 25, 2010). "Arizona immigration law ripples through history, U.S. politics". *The Arizona Republic*. Accessed online at <http://www.azcentral.com/arizonarepublic/news/articles/2010/07/25/20100725immigration-law-history-politics.html?nclick_check=1>]

[cvi] Archibold, Randal C. (April 24, 2010). "U.S.'s Toughest Immigration Law Is Signed in Arizona". *The New York Times*: p. 1. Accessed online at <http://www.nytimes.com/2010/04/24/us/politics/24immig.html?adxnnl=1&ref=us&adxnnlx=1363042965-pchvbkeOWmu+dDe2JaadeA>

[cvii] Cooper, Jonathan J. (April 26, 2010). "Ariz.

immigration law target of protest". Associated Press. MSNBC. Accessed Online at <http://www.nbcnews.com/id/36768649/#.UT5kDdH wLDY>